I AM A TIGER

Steve Macleod

MEDIA ENHANCED BOOKS
AV2 BY WEIGL
ADDED VALUE • AUDIO VISUAL

www.av2books.com

AV² provides enriched content that supplements and complements this book. Weigl's AV² books strive to create inspired learning and engage young minds in a total learning experience.

Your AV² Media Enhanced books come alive with...

Audio
Listen to sections of the book read aloud.

Key Words
Study vocabulary, and complete a matching word activity.

Video
Watch informative video clips.

Quizzes
Test your knowledge.

Embedded Weblinks
Gain additional information for research.

Slide Show
View images and captions, and prepare a presentation.

Go to **www.av2books.com**, and enter this book's unique code.

BOOK CODE

C 2 5 4 6 8 9

AV² by Weigl brings you media enhanced books that support active learning.

Try This!
Complete activities and hands-on experiments.

... and much, much more!

Published by AV² by Weigl
350 5th Avenue, 59th Floor New York, NY 10118
Website: www.av2books.com www.weigl.com

Macleod, Steve.
 Tiger / Steve Macleod.
   p. cm. -- (I am)
 ISBN 978-1-61690-853-9 (hardcover : alk. paper) -- ISBN 978-1-61690-854-6 (softcover : alk. paper)
 1. Tiger--Juvenile literature. I. Title.
 QL737.C23M1847 2011
 599.756--dc22
        2010052416

Printed in the United States of America in North Mankato, Minnesota
1 2 3 4 5 6 7 8 9 0 15 14 13 12 11

052011
WEP37500

Project Coordinator: Aaron Carr
Art Director: Terry Paulhus

Weigl acknowledges Getty Images as the primary image supplier for this title.

I AM A TIGER

In this book, I will teach you about

- myself

- my food

- my home

- my family

and much more!

I am a tiger.

I am the biggest cat
in the world.

I see in the dark six times better than people.

9

I can jump
from one side of a street
to the other.

I eat up to
77 pounds of food
in one meal.

13

I hide the food
I do not finish.

I have a roar
that people can hear
from 2 miles away.

I sleep under trees
or in water.

18

I have pretty stripes on my fur.

I am a tiger.

TIGER FACTS

This page provides more detail about the interesting facts found in the book. Simply look for the corresponding page number to match the fact.

Pages 4-5

I am a tiger. Tigers live in the forests, swamps, and grasslands of Russia and Asia. They have dark stripes that cover their body, head, and tail. A tiger's tail also has black rings on it. Each tiger has its own unique pattern, as no two tigers have the same set of stripes.

Pages 6-7

Tigers are the biggest cats in the world. They are even bigger than lions. The largest tiger can grow to 13 feet (4 meters) long, including its tail, and weigh about 660 pounds (300 kilograms). That is about the same weight as 2,200 baseballs.

Pages 8-9

Tigers can see in the dark six times better than people.
A tiger's eyes let in more light than a person's eyes. This helps tigers see at night. This is when they hunt for their food. Hunting at night helps tigers sneak up on other animals.

Pages 10–11

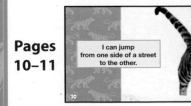

Tigers can jump from one side of a street to the other. That is a distance of 33 feet (10 m). Tigers use their jumping ability to catch their food. They hide in tall grass or shadows, and jump from their hiding place to catch other animals.

Pages 12–13

Tigers can eat 77 pounds (35 kg) of food in one meal. This is about the weight of a German shepherd. Tigers eat so much at one time because they go a long time between meals. It can take a tiger 10 to 20 tries before finally catching food. This can take a few days, or sometimes, it can take up to a week.

Pages 14–15

Tigers hide the food they do not finish. They hide their leftover food under leaves, sticks, and rocks. Tigers do this so other animals do not steal their food and they can eat more when they are hungry again.

Pages 16–17

Tigers roar loud enough to be heard 2 miles (3 km) away. That is a distance of 35 football fields or 40 city blocks. A tiger roars loudly after it has caught a large animal. Tigers have different roars to say different things. They also speak to one another by meowing, hissing, purring, growling, and snarling.

Pages 18–19

Tigers rest under trees or in water. This helps them stay cool and save energy. Tigers need to save their energy, so they do not have to eat as much. Tigers mostly rest during the daytime and can sleep up to 20 hours a day.

Pages 20–21

Tigers have pretty stripes on their fur. For many years, tigers were hunted for their fur and other body parts. Tigers are now an endangered species. Many countries have made laws to protect tigers. There are about 3,200 tigers left in the world.

WORD LIST

Research has shown that as much as 65 percent of all written material published in English is made up of 300 words. These 300 words cannot be taught using pictures or learned by sounding them out. They must be recognized by sight. This book contains 36 common sight words to help young readers improve their reading fluency and comprehension. This book also teaches young readers several important content words, such as proper nouns. These words are paired with pictures to aid in learning and improve understanding.

Page	Sight Words	Page	Content Words
4	a, am, I	4	tiger
6	am, big, I, in, the	6	cat, world
8	better, I, in, people, see, six, than, the	8	dark, times
10	a, can, from, I, jump, of, one, other, to, the	10	side, street
12	eat, food, I, in, of, one, to, up	12	meal, pound
14	do, food, I, not, the	14	finish, hide
16	a, away, can, from, have, hear, I, people, that, two	16	mile, roar
18	I, in, or, sleep, tree, under, water	18	
20	a, am, have, I, my, on, pretty	20	fur, stripe, tiger